Easy Do

3 Fruit Pie Recipes

Apple, Cherry, Crisp Persimmon
(Short Report – 24 pages)

Food and Nutrition Series

Joyce Zborower, M.A.

ISBN-13: 978-1515313267
ISBN-10: 1515313263

Joyce Zborower, M.A.

Table of Contents

3 Fruit Pie Recipes   1

Table of Contents   3

Flaky Pastry Pie Crust   5

Cinnamon Apple Pie   7

Tart Cherry Pie   9

Crisp Persimmon Pie   11

Recipe Excerp   12

One Last Thing Before You Go   14

Recipe Books   15

   Recommended Books   16

--AUDIO-BOOKS   16

--AUDIO-BOOK GAME GUIDES   16

--FOOD AND NUTRITION RELATED BOOKS   17

-- HEALTH & FITNESS/EXERCISE BOOKS   18

-- MYSTERIES/SHORT STORIES   19

-- CRAFTS BOOKS   19

-- SELF-HELP BOOKS   19

-- CHILDREN'S BOOKS   20

-- Español Libros (Spanish language Books)   20

-- Other Recommended Books   21

   Romance Books by Nicole Ann Drak   21

How to Make
Flaky Pastry Pie Crust

For 8" or 9" double-crust pie
1 1/2 cups white, enriched flour (sifted)
1/2 tsp salt
1/2 cup shortening
4 – 5 T cold water

For 10" double crust pie
2 cups white, enriched flour (sifted)
1/2 tsp salt
2/3 cup shortening
6 – 7 T cold water

(1) Sift together the flour and salt. Add 1/2 of the shortening. Use both hands. Scoop the flour mixture up through your fingers while running your thumb across your fingers to break up the shortening and incorporate it into the flour mixture until the flour mixture looks like corn meal. Add remaining shortening and continue running your thumb across your fingers until the pieces look like small peas.

(2) Sprinkle cold water over a small section of flour mixture a tablespoon at a time. Gently mix with fork. Push this to one side of the bowl and do another section. Push this toward moistened section. Repeat till all flour is moistened. Gather up the mass with your fingers and mush it together to make a ball. Let rest several minutes.

(3) Divide dough in half; form two balls. Cover one with towel to keep it moist. Flatten one slightly and roll out on lightly floured pastry cloth. Always roll from center out to edges. If edges split, pinch together and continue rolling. Use light strokes.

(4) Place pie plate upside down over dough. Pick up plate and pastry cloth and flip it over. Gently ease pastry into sides of pie plate. Gently trim excess pastry with knife.

(5) Fill with pie filling.

(6) Roll out other dough ball. Roll dough onto rolling pin and unroll onto pie top. Trim leaving extra dough to turn under bottom crust edge and pinch together to make a decorative edge that holds in the filling.

Cinnamon Apple Pie

The tantalizing aroma of cinnamon wafts through your house as this dessert cooks. You'll have a hard time waiting for it to come out of the oven. Let it cool somewhat, but cutting it warm and eating it with a large scoop of vanilla ice cream . . . is heaven.

Pre-heat oven (400°F)
Here's what you'll need to have on hand:
   -- Flaky Pastry for 2 crust, 9" pie

   -- Filling for pie
   5 – 7 tart green Granny Smith apples – peeled, cored, and sliced thin
   3/4 – 1 cup sugar
   2 tablespoons white whole wheat flour
   Small pinch of salt
   1 tsp cinnamon – a good aromatic variety
   1/4 tsp nutmeg
..... 1 T lemon juice or grated lemon peel (optional if apples aren't very tart)
   2 T unsalted butter
.....a little milk in a glass

Fill a 9" pie plate with peeled, cored, thinly sliced Granny Smith apples. Taste the apples and decide whether or not to use the lemon. Mix sugar, flour, salt, cinnamon, and nutmeg; sprinkle over apples. Dot with butter. Adjust top crust; pinch top and bottom crusts together; cut the top to allow steam to escape.

Dip a pastry brush in the milk and brush the top crust and the edges. Sprinkle sugar from a spoon over the top; then sprinkle with a little extra cinnamon. Don't use too much cinnamon. Bake in hot oven (400°F) 50 minutes.

Tart Cherry Pie

This is a delicious lattice-crust pie that will have your mouth watering from the minute you stick it in the oven. Cut it warm and serve it with a scoop of vanilla ice cream.

Pre-heat oven (450°F)
Here's what you'll need:
    -- Flaky Pastry for 2 crust, 9" pie

    -- Filling for pie
3/4 cup cherry juice
3/4 cup sugar
1 1/2 T quick-cooking tapioca
Pinch salt
2 1/2 cups canned drained pitted tart red cherries*
*Or . . . 2 1/2 cups thawed drained frozen tart dark red cherries
    1 T butter

Combine the juice, sugar, tapioca, salt, and cherries. Set aside for 20 minutes. Fill 9" pie plate with pastry crust. Pour in cherry mixture. Dot with butter.

Roll out top crust and slice into 1/2" strips. Lay the strips, lattice-style, over the cherry mixture. Crimp the edges high to keep the juice from boiling over. Bake at 450°F for 10 minutes. Reduce heat to 350°F and continue cooking for about 30 minutes. Let cool somewhat; slice and enjoy!

And our final recipe. . .

Crisp **Persimmon Pie**

This is a fantastically delicious fruit pie! My husband had gone to a psychology conference in California one summer and while there, visited with some old friends who just happened to grow persimmons. He came home with a basket of ripe persimmons and this yummy family recipe that they shared with him. I don't believe it's ever been published before.

Pre-heat oven (375°F)
Here's what you'll need to have on hand:
   -- Flaky Pastry for 2 crust, 9" pie

   -- Filing for pie:
   1 1/2 T quick-cooking tapioca
   1/3 to 1/2 cup sugar
   1/4 tsp EACH (I use more!)
      Grated lemon peel
      Grated orange peel
      Ground cinnamon
   2 T lemon juice
   4 cups peeled, sliced ***crisp*** persimmons

Mix together the quick-cooking tapioca and sugar. Add remaining ingredients. Let stand 15 minutes.

Bake on lowest rack in oven at 375°F for 50 – 55 minutes. Cool and enjoy!

Recipe Excerpt: : from *Delicious Dinner and Dessert Pie* — **The most delicious savory and sweet pie recipes for dinner and dessert in tender, flaky pie crust you can easily make at home — includes both gluten free pie crust and wheat based pie crust**

Delicious Dinner and Dessert Pie provides 102 pages of mouth watering pies – all kinds of pies! If you like the three pies here, you'll absolutely **love** *Delicious Dinner and Dessert Pie.*

As I write this (September), the Holidays are right around the corner. Fall is here. The trees are turning yellow and red and orange. Pumpkins are getting fat in the fields. Citrus is ripening on the trees. We're beginning to look forward to the sights and sounds and aromas of fresh baked foods for Halloween and Thanksgiving and Christmas. A lot of those luscious aromas are the result of fresh baked pies cooking in the oven. And that's what this book – ***Delicious Dinner and Dessert Pie*** – is all about.

For Halloween, we have delicious pumpkin pie with its cinnamon aroma and its distinct pumpkin flavor that can be enhanced with cold, creamy vanilla ice cream. For Thanksgiving, we have chicken pie and chicken pot pie which can so easily be turned into turkey pie or turkey pot pies just by using some of your left-over turkey instead of chicken. Christmas desserts can be anything from fresh fruit pies in tender, flaky double crusts that are beautifully golden brown to single pie crust meringue or cream or chiffon pies whose aromas make your taste buds tingle as you bend over them to get the greatest pleasure.

Some of our other desserts include:
    Lemon meringue pie recipes
    Apple pie recipes with their distinct sugar and cinnamon aroma

Cherry pie recipe
Black bottom pie with its special Jamaican rum flavor
And various cream and chiffon pies
for your sweet pie recipe collection.

We also give you savory pies including vegetable pies, meat pies, chicken pies, and fish pie recipes for your main meal including:
Shepherds' pie
Chicken pie which could easily become a double pie crust turkey pie
Tuna bake with a cheese swirl topping
Halibut fisherman's pie
and others.

If any of these pie recipes capture your interest, click the buy button now for *Delicious Dinner and Dessert Pie* now. You can be making any of these delicious dinner pies and/or dessert pie recipes within minutes.

One Last Thing Before You Go

Thank you for purchasing *3 Fruit Pie Recipes* – apple, cherry, crisp persimmon.
If you enjoyed it and found it useful, would you take a few minutes and write a short review on its Amazon page? Your opinion is important to me and I do read all messages and use your ideas to help improve work going forward.

Also, please let your friends who also enjoy baking know about it on Facebook and Twitter? They will thank you. . . as will I.

Best ever,
Joyce Zborower

Recipe Books

Delicious Dinner and Dessert Pie – The most delicious savory and sweet pie recipes in tender, flaky pie crust you can make at home – includes gluten free pie crust and wheat-based pie crust

13 Easy Tomato Recipes – nature's lycopene rich superfood for heart health and cancer protection

3 Fruit Pie Recipes – apple, cherry, crisp persimmon

BBQ Spare Ribs Recipe – with homemade honey BBQ sauce

Recommended Books

--AUDIO-BOOKS

The Truth about Olive Oil – Benefits, Curing Methods, Remedies

Signs of Vitamin B12 Deficiencies – Who's at Risk – Why – What Can Be Done

No Work Urban Front Yard Vegetable Gardening Simplified – for in-ground, raised or container gardening

Homebrew Beer – Experience tantalizing tastes from unique beer making ingredients by Eric Andrews

Sell Your Work – Report: How to Turn Your Craft into Your Business

How to Fight Depression – 9 Case Studies by John F. Walsh, M.S. and Joyce Zborower, M.A.

My Cushings Journey – A True Story by Karen Rhodes

Chemotherapy Relief – Chemotherapy research to protect you from chemo side effects

Basic Ab Workouts Give You Sexy Flat Abs – Your one stop flat abs resource – by Michael Weston

Mango Muffin Murder – Island Kitchen Cozy Culinary Mystery by Emma Johns

--AUDIO-BOOK GAME GUIDES

Piano Tiles Game: Cheats, Online, Mod, Apk, Download Guide – HiddenStuff Entertainment

Subway Surfers: Tips, Cheats, Tricks, & Strategies – HiddenStuff Entertainment

8 Ball Pool Game: How to Download for Android, PC, iOS, Kindle + Tips – HiddenStuff Entertainment

The Sims Free Play Game Guide – HiddenStuff Entertainment

Call of Duty Black Ops 3 xBox Game Guide Unofficial BY THE YEW

Clash Royale Game Decks, Strategy, Reddit Download Guide Unofficial by Chala Dar/HiddenStuff Entertainment

Animation Throwdown the Quest for Cards Game Guide Unofficial BY THE YEW

Roblox Unofficial Guide by HSE Games

Minecraft PS4 Edition Game Guide Unofficial by HSE Games

Plants Vs Zombies Garden Warfare Xbox One Game Guide Unofficial BY THE YEW

Plants Vs Zombies Garden Warfare Pc Game Guide Unofficial BY THE YEW

Plants vs Zombies Garden Warfare 2 Game – PC, Review, Xbox, Guide, Unofficial: Get Tons of Coins & Beat Levels by Chala Dar/HiddenStuff Entertainment

Plants vs Zombies Garden Warfare 2 Game Xbox, Pc, Download Guide Unofficial by Chala Dar

--FOOD AND NUTRITION RELATED BOOKS

Paleo Slow Cooker Cookbook – 31 low carb and/or gluten free paleo slow cooker recipes for busy folks who love homemade food by Julie A. Anderson

25 Crockpot Meals with MEAT –Delicious, easy, healthy Crockpot Meals with Meat (beef and pork) in 3 Steps or Less by Julie A. Anderson

25 Crockpot Meals with CHICKEN – Delicious, easy, healthy Crockpot Chicken Recipes in 3 Steps or Less by Julie A. Anderson

25 Crockpot Meals for BREAKFAST – Delicious, easy, healthy Crockpot Breakfast Recipes in 3 Steps or Less by Julie A. Anderson

75 Crockpot Meals Cookbook in 3 Steps or Less by Julie A. Anderson – 3 book set
Meat – Chicken -- Breakfast

Delicious Dinner and Dessert Pie – Pie recipes for quick and easy pies and pie crust -- by Julie A. Anderson

Homebrew Beer – How to brew beer right the first time and experience tantalizing tastes from unique beer making ingredients -- by Eric Andrews

No Work Vegetable Gardening – for in-ground, raised, or container gardening

3 Fruit Pie Recipes – apple, cherry, crisp persimmon

How to Eat Healthy – foods to eat . . . foods to avoid – clean eating made simple

Extra Virgin Olive Oil Explainedl – Organic Olive Oil Benefits for Skin, Hair and Nutrition,

External Uses of Extra Virgin Olive Oil – Folk Remedies ... Body Lotions ... Pet Treatments

Signs of Vitamin B12 Deficiencies – Who's at Risk – Why – What Can Be Done

13 Easy Tomato Recipes – nature's lycopene rich superfood for heart health and cancer protection

BBQ Spare Ribs Recipe – with homemade honey BBQ sauce

-- HEALTH & FITNESS/EXERCISE BOOKS – by

Michael Weston

Basic Ab Workouts Give You Sexy Flat Abs --- by Michael Weston

Ab Workouts For Skinny Guys Who Want To Build Some Muscle and Turn Some Heads Even If You've Never Been Able To Do That With Other Workout Programs ---- by Michael Weston

-- MYSTERIES/SHORT STORIES

Mango Muffin Murder – Island Kitchen Cozy Culinary Mystery by Emma Johns – Book1 Jamaica Series
Murder by Mistake -- Island Kitchen Cozy Culinary Mystery by Emma Johns – Book2 Jamaica Series
The Trust – a cautionary tale
Little Mysteries – a short story

-- CRAFTS BOOKS – by Joyce Zborower

Handcrafted Jewelry Step by Step – 6 advanced and intermediate original designs
Handcrafted Jewelry Photo Gallery – cast jewelry -- fabricated jewelry
Wire Jewelry Photo Gallery – Original designs
Creations in Wood Photo Gallery – jewelry boxes, screens, storage ideas
Bargello Quilts Photo Gallery – quilt wall hangings
Bargello Train Quilt – cutting and sewing instructions
Sell Your Work – how to turn your craft into your business

-- SELF-HELP BOOKS – by Joyce Zborower. M.A. and/or John F. Walsh, M.S.

Chemotherapy Relief – Chemotherapy research results to protect you from chemo side effects
Psychology of Success – RESEARCH -- How to have success when trying to change how you look
Different Types of Depression – Characteristics and Treatments by Joyce Zborower. M.A. and John F. Walsh, M.S.
How to Fight Depression – 9 case studies ---- by John F. Walsh

Clinical Psychology – A Professional Perspective – memoirs and experiences – John F. Walsh, M.S.

-- CHILDREN'S BOOKS – by Joyce Zborower

Baby Pics Counting and Number Book -- 1-13 The numbers are in numerals and words with lots of photos of babies.
Christmas ABCs – cute animal illustrations

Most of the above are also available as print-on-demand paperback editions. Also:

Grandma's No Work Vegetable Gardening – (paperback edition) same as *No Work Vegetable Gardening* except the photos are B&W and the price is lower.

-- Español Libros (Spanish language Books)

-- by Joyce Zborower and M. Angelica Brunell S.
Haga click aquí para ir a mi página de Amazon
Pequeños Misterios – cuento
Joyas Artesanales Galeria de fotos – Joyas fundidas – joyas forjadas
Joyas de Alambre - Galería de fotos – Diseños originales
Creaciones en Madera- Galería de fotos – joyeros, biombos, ideas de almacenaje
Quilts Estilo Bargello - Galería de fotos – tapices de quilt
Bargello Quilt de Tren – instrucciones para cortar y coser
Vende tuTrabajo – como transformar tu arte en negocio
Signos de deficiencia de vitamina B12 -- Quén esta en riesgo – Por qué – Qué puede hacerse
Huerto sin Esfuerzo – para jardinería en el suelo, elevada o en contenedor

La Verdad Acerca del Aceite de Oliva – beneficios, métodos de curación, remedios

3 Recetas de Pie de Fruta -- Manzana, Cereza, Caqui fresco

13 Recetas de Tomate Fáciles -- Superalimentos de la naturaleza ricos en licopeno para la salud del corazón y protección contra el cáncer

Receta de Chuletas de Cerdo en Barbacoa -- con salsa casera de barbacoa con miel

Fotos de Bebés Libro de Números y de Contar De 2 a 5 años – 1 – 13

ABCs de Navidad – Para niños de 2 a 5 años

-- Other Recommended Books

Romance Books by Nicole Ann Drake

**** WARNING ****
These books by Nicole Ann Drake contain sexually explicit scenes and adult language. They may be considered offensive to some readers. These books are for sale to adults ONLY.
(Must be 18 or older.)

# # #

If you enjoyed this book, leave a review on its page.

Joyce Zborower, M.A.

11652102R00015